THE XXL AIR FRYER COOKBOOK FOR UK

Quick and Easy Recipes for Family and Friends incl. A Collection of Desserts and Side Dishes

Food Club UK

ISBN – 9798717212243

Table of Contents

Introduction

Oiled-soaked, fried foods were a thing back in the day. However, when we started experiencing the many health impacts that came with these types of foods, things started to change. Most of us had to switch to something else, such as boiled vegetables and lean meats. It wasn't until Philips Electronics patented the air fryer that most of us got back to enjoying crispy, fried dishes.

The air fryer as a kitchen appliance has made cooking times a lot faster. It also helps us to create innovative foods. In addition, with every household rushing to furnish their kitchens with one of these magical cooking appliances, we can only expect to discover even more fresh and tasty recipes.

What Is an Air Fryer?

An air fryer is a cooking appliance that gives similar results to a deep fryer but with little or no oil at all. Over the past few years, air fryer usage has surged all over the world.

Today, you can fry all kinds of dishes with an air fryer from roasted vegetables to French fries and baked cookies.

How Do Air Fryers Work?

Ironically, an air fryer doesn't work by frying – the same way a deep fryer does – but more like a hot air convection oven fryer. The food in the air fryer is suspended and held in position by a perforated cooking basket. The air fryer has a fan that blows hot air around the food. This force produces a convection effect that cooks the food, making it brown and crisp.

The air fryer maintains the internal temperature at 160°C which is enough to cook breaded foods, such as frozen marinated chicken tenders or unbreaded foods, such as French fries.

The air fryer cooks faster and can distribute heat more evenly compared to how many other cooking appliances work. You'll also discover that preheating does not apply to all air fryers; some don't require it, which makes them cook food faster.

Unlike conventional ovens, air fryers are convenient in all seasons because they don't heat the house in warmer climates.

Types of Air Fryers

Here are some of the main types of air fryers.

Paddle-Type Air Fryer

Paddle-type air fryers save you the hassle of pulling out the food from the air fryer to stir it. They are designed with a paddle inside the air fryer, which moves through the cooking basket to circulate the hot air with ease and uniformity.

In most paddle-type air fryers, you can easily remove the paddle while cooking if the paddle gets in the way.

Basket-Type Air Fryer

Basket-type air fryers cook food in a basket. The basket is perforated to enable hot air to get through and around your food. You may still need to stir a few times during the cooking process.

That said, because of the perforations, you cannot cook saucy or soupy dishes with these basket-type air fryers.

Although cheaper than paddle-type air fryers, the basket-type air fryer requires more frequent cleaning, especially depending on the recipes you're exploring.

Countertop Convection Oven

Convection countertop air fryers heat food through the convection effect. Some models have an air fryer setting which enables you to get similar results to standard air fryers. Their primary advantage is that they offer more versatility than other types of air fryers.

They are not only larger but have multiple cooking options to help you cook a wider range of recipes. The wire racks in the middle give you the option to cook multiple items at the same time.

What Can You Cook in an Air Fryer?

When the air fryer hit the mainstream market, most households thought it was just another appliance to warm food, prepare a snack, cook chips or fry frozen foods, like chicken tenders. Nothing describes underutilisation more than that.

An air fryer is not for convenience meals alone – this cookbook will show you how you can prepare your food items from scratch.

Think of anything you've ever baked or roasted in the traditional oven, from steak, lamb chops and pork chops, burgers to chicken breasts. Whether breaded or not, the air fryer can cook them to the perfect temperature, just as juicy and tender as you like them.

Vegetables

Are you a fan of oven-fried vegetables or vegetable stuffing? The good news is that air fryers are great at cooking vegetables. With a little spritz of avocado or olive oil, an air fryer will get your vegetables brown and crisp and ready to satisfy your taste buds.

The air fryer cooks most vegetables within 10 minutes. Try out broccoli, mushrooms, asparagus and baked potatoes in your air fryer and you will not be disappointed. This cookbook contains some tasty vegetable recipes that you should be eager to try out.

Frozen Finger Foods

The air fryer is, without a doubt, a kitchen 'jack of all trades' when it comes to preparing frozen food. You can use it to prepare any frozen finger foods that you want to taste deep-fried.

Frozen mozzarella sticks, chips, and chickens cook perfectly in an air fryer. This air fryer cookbook has some secret frozen finger food recipes that you shouldn't miss.

Besides finger foods, an air fryer is perfect for heating frozen leftovers. It revives their juiciness and crispiness, thus making them tastier.

Homemade Finger Foods

Do you like experimenting with new recipes in your kitchen? There is no better appliance to try your homemade finger foods than the air fryer. It is turning out to be the simplest and cleanest appliance for making homemade sides and snacks. You can try out sweet potato fries, air fryer pickles or the air fryer papas Rellenas.

Chicken, Fish and Meat

Despite the carb-filled foods mentioned earlier, you can use your air fryer to cook dishes packed with plentiful proteins.

This includes beefy meals, pork, ham, fish and chicken recipes. The air-fried spicy roasted chicken drumsticks and air fried chicken tenders are interesting recipes you have to try out.

There are also healthier options such as the air fryer keto meatballs for keto diet lovers.

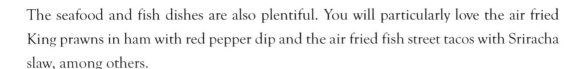

The seafood and fish dishes are also plentiful. You will particularly love the air fried King prawns in ham with red pepper dip and the air fried fish street tacos with Sriracha slaw, among others.

Some Baked Goods

With accessories such as muffin and loaf tins, you can bake almost everything with an air fryer. This cookbook contains mouth-watering single-serve desserts including chocolate brownies, chocolate profiteroles, and apple fritters.

The baked goods made in an air fryer are delicious and cooked to perfection. It is an all-seasons baked goods appliance, which enables you to bake winter air-fried peppermint lava cakes or Nutella doughnuts for any time of the year.

Bring out the chef in you with these great air fryer recipes and get the full value from your air fryer.

What Should I Look for in an Air Fryer?

Is your air fryer ready for the great cooking experience you're about to obtain? How will you know that your air fryer has all it takes to turn you into a chief chef?

Here are some of the factors and features you should look for in air fryers in the market;

Loading: Some air fryers are designed with front drawers to load and unload the food while others come with a flip-top lid. The drawer style models happen to be a top pick among expert chefs because it offers safety and convenience.

Ease of use: The air fryer controls should be simple to operate and understand. Not everyone has the time to go through the user manual, although it's highly recommended that you do. Your air fryer of choice should also provide some ease of detaching and cleaning of the cooking basket.

Controls: The majority of air fryer models in the market can set temperatures up to 200°C. However, it is also likely to find one with just a single temperature setting. You may want to go for one that also has reheat buttons for your leftovers and a pre-set button as well.

Functionality: When it comes to the choice of an air fryer, functionality can be a game-changer. Does your air fryer enable you to pause the cooking so you can flip, stir and turn your food? Some models will allow you to reset both the temperature and time of cooking.

Size: Air fryers should be big enough to cook food for 4 people. Most models can only cook for 2 at a go, therefore, requiring you to cook in batches for more people. That said, there are new models with an oven toaster that enable you to save your countertop space by replacing the toaster.

How to Clean an Air Fryer

The best thing about an air fryer is that it uses a fraction of the grease a traditional fryer does. This means you'll still enjoy the crispy goodness, but healthier.

However, since you're cooking food with some amount of grease, you have some cleaning to do. This allows you to remove food particles that are stuck on the air fryer.

You may be comfortable with the standard cleaning using soap and water but this can only do so much in terms of cleaning the baked-on grease. The homemade mixture of vinegar and baking soda can provide some assistance as it helps remove gunk. However, this will take up to 30 minutes to take effect.

It is advisable NOT to use metal utensils, abrasive sponge or steel wool to remove baked-on gunk from the air fryer. These items can cause a lot more harm than good to the non-stick coating in your air fryer.

An all-purpose cleaner might help solve the problem of cleaning your air fryer after frequent use. These non-abrasive formulas are designed to remove grease from the air fryer cooking basket and trays. They also eliminate grime and stains from the outside and inside of your appliance.

Directions for Cleaning an Air Fryer

It is best practice to wash the cooking basket, pans and trays after every use. You can do this using the instructions provided below.

- ➷ Prepare your air fryer for cleaning by turning it off and unplugging it from the socket. Let it cool before you start cleaning. To make it cool faster, remove the cooking basket and pan from the main unit.

- Wipe the outside surface by mixing the all-purpose cleaner in a regular-sized cup of water (or as directed) in a spray bottle. Spray it on a clean damp cloth and wipe the outside surface with the cloth.

- Clean the inside surface of the main unit by spraying the undiluted all-purpose cleaner on a clean damp cloth and use the cloth to wipe the interior. Wipe again using a plain damp clean piece of cloth.

- Clean the coil by wiping down the heating element with the pure all-purpose cleaner to remove any stains, oil or residue. Use a plain damp cloth for the second time.

- Wash the pans, tray and cooking basket in a dishwasher or by hand. Ensure the components are dishwasher safe before washing them. To remove baked-on grease from the removable parts, mix the all-purpose cleaner with hot water in the sink then soak the parts for 10 minutes. Remove the soaked debris/residue/grease using a scrub brush then rinse to clean. Dry the parts completely before returning them to the main unit of the air fryer.

General Ways of using an Air Fryer

Preparing to Air Frying

- As you prepare to start air frying, ensure you place your air fryer in the right place in the kitchen. The best practice is to place it on a level surface and preferably a heat resistant worktop. Still, on the positioning of the air fryer, maintain some 5-inch of space behind the air fryer. where the exhaust vent is placed.

- Always preheat the air fryer before you add any food inside. To do this you only need to turn on the appliance and set it to the temperature you'll be cooking at then set the timer for 3 minutes. This will preheat the air fryer making it ready for use.

- Air frying requires the right set of accessories. Invest in some worthy accessories for your new favourite kitchen appliance. Luckily, some oven-safe accessories are also air fryer safe; therefore, if you had some for your oven, you may not need to purchase new ones for the air fryer. The pan, besides being air fryer safe, should also be able to fit inside the main unit of the air fryer.

- Before you start air frying, ensure to get a kitchen spray bottle if you don't have one already. Spraying cooking oil is easier, safer and less messy than brushing or drizzling. It also allows you to use a little oil.

- Another important small but significant item you'll need in preparation for your air frying episodes is an aluminium foil sling. It is going to help place in and take out accessory pieces in the air fryer basket. You can make one yourself by folding a piece of aluminium foil into a 2-inch wide, 24-inch long strip. Place the cake pan on the foil. When you hold the ends of the strip, you can lower the pan into the baking basket or you can also pull it out of the basket the same way.

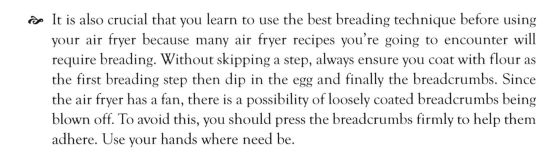

   ❧ It is also crucial that you learn to use the best breading technique before using your air fryer because many air fryer recipes you're going to encounter will require breading. Without skipping a step, always ensure you coat with flour as the first breading step then dip in the egg and finally the breadcrumbs. Since the air fryer has a fan, there is a possibility of loosely coated breadcrumbs being blown off. To avoid this, you should press the breadcrumbs firmly to help them adhere. Use your hands where need be.

With these tips, you're now set to start air frying but before that, you might also want to learn about best practices during the actual air frying.

While you are Air Frying

   ❧ Ensure you add water to the drawer beneath the air fryer whenever you're cooking fatty dishes such as sausage or bacon. This is done to prevent the grease from overheating or smoking.

   ❧ Avoid overcrowding the cooking basket since this prevents the food from evenly browning and crisping. Be patient and cook small batches at a time.

   ❧ Remember to flip and turn the food halfway through the cooking to ensure it browns evenly on all sides.

   ❧ It is okay to open the air fryer to check for doneness. This does not interrupt the cooking process in any way – in most cases, the air fryer will simply continuing timing and heating from where it left off.

   ❧ When cooking a sandwich, the fan might blow up the top slices. You can hold the sandwich in place by using a toothpick to pin down the top slices.

   ❧ Shaking the air fryer cooking basket is also a common practice when air frying. It is done to redistribute the ingredients and ensure they all come to brown and crisp evenly.

After Air Frying

When you're certain the food is fully cooked, remove the air fryer basket from the drawer before you turn the food out. Inverting the basket while it is locked in the main unit will dump all the rendered fat onto the plate with the air fried food.

What's more, don't be quick to discard the juices in the air fryer drawer after removing the cooking basket. The juices that collect in the drawer beneath may include marinades, which if not greasy, can be used as a flavourful sauce. Even if it is greased, degreasing and reducing it in a small saucepan over heat for a few minutes helps concentrate the flavour.

Remember the air fryer cleaning tips in the previous section? Put them into use after every air frying exercise. However, what you didn't know is that you can use the air fryer to dry itself. After washing the basket, pans, trays and drawers, slot them into the main unit and turn the air fryer on for 3 minutes. This should do the magic of drying better than any towel.

Re-heating Foods in an Air Fryer

Re-heating food leftovers vary significantly. Most people prefer to re-heat at 175°C, long enough to get the food heated to a food-safe temperature of 165°C. It is important to keep this in mind when re-heating beef, chicken and pork.

Trouble-shooting

As you prepare to start air frying, remember that there will always be uncertainties. For instance, the food may not be crispy enough or you may observe white smoke coming out of your air fryer. What will you do in such instances?

Here are some troubleshooting tips to help you out:

- Ensure your food is not overcrowded since this prevents it from not being crispy enough. Also, ensure you're using just a little oil, especially when cooking fries or regular chips.

- When you observe white smoke, add water to the drawer beneath the air fryer. The smoke indicates the burning of grease that has drained into the drawer.

- In some cases, instead of the white smoke, you might observe black smoke. This usually means some food may have blown up and stuck onto the heating element and ended up burning. No need to panic, all you have to do is turn off the air fryer and look at the heating element inside the fryer. Use a fork or spoon to remove the stuck food.

Air fryers are designed to turn off gradually. This is why you'll observe a delay when you press the turn off button. The air fryer fan will continue to blow some air but this will only last for a few more seconds - just be patient and let it turn off.

Air Fryer Recipes

SIDE DISHES AND VEGETABLES

CRISPY POTATO SKIN WEDGES

```
NUTRITIONAL INFORMATION
CALORIES: 129KCAL
PROTEIN: 2.3G
CARBOHYDRATES: 19G
FAT: 5.3G
COOKING TIME: 40 MINUTES
SERVES: FOUR
```

INGREDIENTS

- 6 medium-sized Maris Piper potatoes
- 2 tablespoons of olive oil
- 1 teaspoon of paprika
- ¼ teaspoon of white salt
- ¼ teaspoon of black pepper

PROCEDURE

1. Scrub the Maris Piper potatoes under a running tap to clean
2. Boil the Maris Piper potatoes in salted water for 40 minutes until they are fork-tender
3. Remove the potatoes from the boiling water to cool them completely (place them in the refrigerator for about 30 minutes.)
4. Mix the black pepper, paprika, white salt and olive oil in a mixing bowl
5. Chop the cooled Maris Piper potatoes into quarters and toss them lightly in the seasonings in the mixing bowl
6. Preheat the air fryer to 200°C
7. Put half of the potato wedges into the basket placing them skin side down. Be careful not to overcrowd them
8. Cook each batch for 15 minutes

FRENCH FRIES

NUTRITIONAL INFORMATION
CALORIES: 312KCAL
CARBS: 32.7G
FAT: 13.7G
PROTEIN: 3.2G
FIBRE: 3G
COOKING TIME: 10 MINUTES
SERVES: 4

INGREDIENTS

- 5 medium-sized Maris Piper potatoes
- 2 tablespoon of olive oil
- 1 pinch sea salt

PROCEDURE

1. Wash and peel the potatoes
2. Cut the peeled potatoes into ½ by 3-inch strips
3. Soak the potato strips in water for no less than 30 minutes
4. Drain the soaked strips and pat dry using a paper towel
5. Proceed to preheat the air fryer to 180°C
6. In a large bowl, mix the strips with oil to coat the potatoes lightly
7. Put the potatoes into a cooking basket and toss into the air fryer then let it cook for 30 minutes to crispiness
8. Shake 2-3 times during cooking

AIR FIRED POTATO CROQUETTES

NUTRITIONAL INFORMATION
CALORIES: 220KCAL
FAT: 8.5G
CARBOHYDRATES: 25.4G
PROTEIN: 10.9G
COOKING TIME: 45 MINUTES
SERVES: 5

INGREDIENTS

For filling

- 3 peeled medium-sized Maris Piper potatoes
- 1 egg yolk
- 60g of parmesan grated cheese
- 2 tablespoons of flour (all-purpose)
- 1 pinch of white salt
- 1 pinch of nutmeg
- 1 pinch of black pepper

For breading

- 2 beaten eggs
- 125g all-purpose flour
- 60g of breadcrumbs
- 2 tablespoon of vegetable cooking oil

PROCEDURE

1. Wash and cut the potatoes into cubes
2. Boil the cubes in salted water for 15 minutes
3. Drain the cubes and mash them finely in a large bowl using a potato masher
4. Cool the mashed potatoes in a refrigerator
5. Mix the cheese, flour, chives and egg yolk
6. Use the salt, nutmeg and black pepper to season
7. Mould the potato filling into golf ball sizes and set them aside

8. Preheat the oven air fryer to 200°C

9. Mix the breadcrumbs with oil and stir to make the mixture crumbly and loose

10. Toss the balls of potato into the flour, then into the eggs and finally into the crumbled breadcrumbs

11. Roll them into balls

12. Firmly press the coating onto the croquettes

13. Put half of the croquettes into the cooking basket

14. Cook each batch for 8 minutes until they turn golden brown

AIR FRIED POTATOES AU GRATIN

NUTRITIONAL INFORMATION

CALORIES: 220KCAL
CARBOHYDRATES: 24G
FIBRE: 1G
PROTEIN: 7G
FAT: 11G
COOKING TIME: 10 MINUTES
SERVES: 3

INGREDIENTS

- 3 peeled Maris Piper potatoes
- 60ml of milk
- 60g of Gruyere grated cheese
- ¼ cup of cream
- ½ teaspoon of nutmeg
- 1 teaspoon of black pepper

PROCEDURE

1. Wash and slice the potatoes thinly
2. Mix the cream and cream in a mixing bowl
3. Use the salt, nutmeg and pepper for seasoning
4. Coat the potato slices with the milk and cream mixture
5. Put the potato slices into a baking tin and toss the rest of the mixture on top of the potatoes
6. Put the baking tin into a cooking basket and place the basket into the air fryer
7. Set the air fryer to 15 minutes and let the gratin bake at 165°C
8. Spread the cheese over the potatoes evenly, then set the timer to 10 minutes and bake again until the gratin turns golden brown

ROSEMARY MARIS PIPER POTATO CRISPS

> NUTRITIONAL INFORMATION
> CALORIES: 120KCAL
> TOTAL FAT: 3 ½G
> CARBOHYDRATES: 20G
> PROTEIN: 2G
> COOKING TIME: 40 MINUTES
> SERVES: 3

INGREDIENTS

- 2 medium-sized Maris Piper potatoes
- 1 tablespoon of olive oil
- 1 teaspoon of chopped rosemary
- 1 pinch of white salt

PROCEDURE

1. Clean the potatoes by scrubbing them under running water
2. Cut the washed potatoes lengthwise and peel
3. Cut into thin slices and put into a bowl of water
4. Soak the potato slices for 30 minutes (ensure to change the water several times)
5. Drain and pat to dryness using a paper towel
6. Preheat the air fryer to 167°C
7. Toss the potatoes into a mixing bowl and mix with olive oil
8. Put them into a cooking basket and let it cook for 30 minutes to golden brown
9. Shake at intervals to ensure the crisps are evenly cooked
10. Toss the cooked crisps into a bowl and mix with rosemary and white salt

GARLIC AND VERMOUTH ROASTED MUSHROOMS

```
NUTRITIONAL INFORMATION
CALORIES: 92KCAL
PROTEIN: 7.2G
FAT: 3.9G
SODIUM: 13MG
COOKING TIME: 30 MINUTES
SERVES: 3
```

INGREDIENTS

- 1kg of dried mushrooms
- 1 tablespoon of goose or duck fat
- 2 tablespoon of herbs de Provence
- 2 tablespoons of French Vermouth
- ½ tablespoon of garlic powder

PROCEDURE

1. Wash the mushrooms and spin-dry them in a salad spinner
2. Cut into quarters and set them aside
3. Put the goose fat into the air fryer and add the garlic powder and herbs de Provence
4. Heat for 2 minutes
5. Stir with a wooden spoon to remove clumps and add the mushrooms
6. Cook for 20 minutes at 175°C
7. Add the French Vermouth and cook for a further 5 minutes

AIR FRIED CAULIFLOWER RICE

```
NUTRITIONAL INFORMATION
CALORIES: 170KCAL
PROTEIN: 16.2G
CARBOHYDRATES: 11.6G
FAT: 7.4G
COOKING TIME: 40 MINUTES
SERVES: 4
```

INGREDIENTS FOR ROUND 1

- ½ block tofu
- 175g diced onions
- 80g diced carrots

- 2 tablespoons soy sauce
- 1 teaspoon turmeric

INGREDIENTS FOR ROUND 2

- 3 large cauliflower heads
- 2 cloves minced garlic
- 60g chopped broccoli
- 60g frozen peas

- 1 tablespoon ginger
- 1 tablespoon rice vinegar
- 1 ½ teaspoon sesame oil

PROCEDURE

1. Crumble the tofu in a large bowl
2. Add to the air fryer with diced onions, carrots, soy sauce and turmeric
3. Cook for 10mins at 170°C, shaking only once
4. Toss the cauliflower, garlic, broccoli, peas, ginger, vinegar and sesame oil in a large bowl
5. Mix well and add into the air fryer, shake well and continue cooking for a further 10 minutes at 170°C

AIR FRIED ASPARAGUS

```
NUTRITIONAL INFORMATION
CALORIES: 94KCAL
PROTEIN: 9G
CARBOHYDRATES: 10.1G
FAT: 3.3G
COOKING TIME: 10 MINUTES
SERVES: 5
```

INGREDIENTS

- 2 tablespoons of olive or avocado oil
- ½ bunch of trimmed asparagus
- 1 pinch of Himalayan salt
- ¼ teaspoon of black pepper

PROCEDURE

1. Place the asparagus in the air fryer
2. Spritz lightly with the olive or avocado oil
3. Add the salt and black pepper
4. Cook for 10 minutes at 200°C
5. Serve immediately

BAKED GARLIC POTATO PARSLEY

```
NUTRITIONAL INFORMATION
CALORIES: 276KCAL
FAT: 20G
CARBOHYDRATES: 24.1G
PROTEIN: 2G
COOKING TIME: 40 MINUTES
SERVES: 4
```

INGREDIENTS

- 4 Maris Piper baking potatoes
- 2 tablespoon of olive oil
- 1 tablespoon white salt
- 1 tablespoon garlic
- 1 teaspoon parsley

PROCEDURE

1. Wash the Maris Piper potatoes
2. Poke the potatoes with a fork to create holes
3. Sprinkle the potatoes with olive, garlic and salt
4. Once the potatoes are evenly coated, place the basket into the air fryer
5. Cook for 35 minutes at 200°C
6. Top with parsley and serve

ROASTED PEPPER ROLLS

NUTRITIONAL INFORMATION
CALORIES: 55KCAL
PROTEIN: 0.8G
CARBOHYDRATES: 5.6G
FAT: 3.5G
COOKING TIME: 20 MINUTES
SERVES: 4

INGREDIENTS

- 2 medium-sized orange, red and yellow bell peppers
- Tapas fork
- Filling as required

PROCEDURE

1. Preheat the air fryer to 180°C
2. Place the bell peppers into the basket and toss the basket into the air fryer
3. Cook for 10 minutes to allow the peppers to roast, until the skin gets slightly charred
4. Cut the bell peppers into half and remove the seeds and skin
5. Use the filling of your choice to stuff the bell peppers and roll them up starting from the narrowest end
6. Use a tapas fork to secure the bell peppers and place them on a platter

APPETIZERS/ENTREES

AIR FRIED CHEESE SOUFFLÉ

NUTRITIONAL INFORMATION
CALORIES: 238KCAL
PROTEIN: 11.9G
CARBOHYDRATES: 15.3G
FAT: 12G
COOKING TIME: 30 MINUTES
SERVES: 5

INGREDIENTS

- 4 whole eggs
- 30g panko breadcrumbs
- 60g cheddar cheese
- 30g dairy butter
- 30g finely grated parmesan cheese
- 60g all-purpose flour
- 350ml milk (preferably skimmed milk)
- 2 tablespoons fine white sugar
- 2 tablespoons olive oil
- ½ tablespoon nutmeg
- ½ tablespoon vanilla extract

PROCEDURE

1. Preheat the air fryer to 167°C
2. Grease the soufflé dishes with olive oil spray
3. Sprinkle the breadcrumbs on the oil greased dishes
4. Melt the butter in a small saucepan
5. Add the all-purpose flour to the melted butter
6. Stir the two ingredients in the saucepan until smooth
7. Transfer the mixture to a small, clean bowl and clean the saucepan
8. Heat the skimmed milk and then add vanilla extract, stirring well
9. Bring the milk and vanilla extract to boil
10. Add the flour and butter mixture into the pan

11. Use a whisk to mix ingredients, ensuring there are no lumps and achieving a smooth consistency
12. Simmer the sauce to thicken it
13. Quickly transfer the saucepan over a bowl of iced water and let it cool for 10 minutes
14. Separate egg whites from egg yolks in a mixing bowl
15. Add the separated egg yolks to the thickened sauce and stir in parmesan and cheddar
16. Add nutmeg for seasoning
17. Whisk another batch of egg whites in a separate bowl until peaks form
18. Use a metal spoon to stir the egg whites gradually into the sauce mixture
19. Distribute the mixture in soufflé dishes and use a knife to even out the tops
20. Place the soufflé dishes into the air fryer basket and cook for 20 minutes
21. Remove from the air fryer and sprinkle some fine sugar on the cooked cheese soufflé

CHEDDAR BACON CROQUETTES

```
NUTRITIONAL INFORMATION
CALORIES: 46KCAL
PROTEIN: 1G
CARBOHYDRATES: 4G
FAT: 3G
COOKING TIME: 50 MINUTES
SERVES: 6
```

INGREDIENTS

For filling

- 450g mature cheese
- 450g thinly sliced bacon

For breading

- 2 beaten eggs
- 125g all-purpose flour
- 125g breadcrumbs
- 4 tablespoons olive oil

PROCEDURE

1. Slice the cheese into 6 equal portions, roughly 25cm x 50cm
2. Wrap two pieces of bacon around each portion of cheese. Ensure you enclose the cheese fully and trim the excess
3. Place the cheesy bacon in the freezer for 6 minutes, until it is firm. Be careful not to freeze it
4. Preheat the air fryer to 200°C
5. Mix the breadcrumbs with oil then stir the mixture to make it crumbly and loose
6. Take the cheesy bacon and dip it into the flour
7. Add the beaten eggs then add breadcrumbs

8. Press the coating to the croquettes firmly
9. Put the croquettes into the cooking basket and toss the basket into the oven air fryer
10. Cook for 8 minutes

Bonus tip: Dip the croquettes into the beaten egg and breadcrumbs to double coat your croquettes. This ensures you don't run out of cheese

CRAB CROQUETTES

```
NUTRITIONAL INFORMATION
CALORIES: 104KCAL
PROTEIN: 6.9G
CARBOHYDRATES: 2.5G
FAT: 7.5G
COOKING TIME: 20 MINUTES
SERVES: 6
```

INGREDIENTS

For filling

- 450g crabmeat
- 2 beaten egg whites
- 30g sour cream
- 30g mayonnaise
- 45g finely chopped red onion
- 45g finely pound red bell pepper

- 2 tablespoon finely chopped celery
- 1 tablespoon olive oil
- ½ teaspoon cayenne pepper
- ½ teaspoon finely chopped parsley
- ¼ teaspoon finely ground chives
- ¼ teaspoon finely ground tarragon

For breading

- 3 beaten eggs
- 125g panko breadcrumbs
- 125g all-purpose flour

- 1 teaspoon olive oil
- ½ teaspoon white salt

PROCEDURE

1. Put a small frying pan over a medium heat then add the olive oil, celery, bell peppers and red onions
2. Cook for about 5 minutes
3. Remove the frying pan from the heat and let it cool

4. Blend the panko breadcrumbs, salt and olive oil in a food processor
5. Add the breadcrumb mixture, beaten eggs and all-purpose flour in three separate bowls
6. In a large mixing bowl, toss together the mayonnaise, sour cream, egg whites and crab meat. Add tarragon, chives and parsley
7. Preheat the air fryer to 200°C
8. Mould the crab meat into golf ball sizes
9. Roll each ball in the flour, then the eggs and finally the breadcrumbs
10. Press the crumbs to croquettes to adhere
11. Carefully place the croquettes into the cooking basket. Do not overcrowd them
12. Cook each batch for 10 minutes

AIR FRYER CHEESEBURGERS

CALORIES: 821KCAL
CARBOHYDRATES: 42.2G
PROTEINS: 54G
FATS: 47.2G
COOKING TIME: 20 MINUTES
SERVING: 4

INGREDIENTS

- 450g minced beef
- 4 hamburger buns
- 4 slices cheddar cheese
- 2 cloves garlic, crushed
- Mayonnaise
- Lettuce
- Thinly sliced red onion
- Sliced tomatoes
- 1 tablespoon low sodium soy sauce
- 1 pinch black pepper

PROCEDURE

1. Combine beef, soy sauce and crushed garlic in a large bowl
2. Shape the beef into 4 burgers then flatten them into 11cm circles
3. Season both sides of the patties with salt
4. Put 2 burgers into the air fryer and cook at 180°C for up to 4 minutes, turning it and cooking the opposite sides for the same amount of time. Do this for the other 2 burgers also
5. Spread hamburger buns with mayonnaise
6. Top with lettuce, then place the burgers inside. Add tomatoes and onions and cover with the bun top.

CHIMICHURRI SKIRT STEAK

```
NUTRITIONAL INFORMATION
CALORIES: 678KCAL
PROTEIN: 27G
CARBOHYDRATES: 14G
FAT: 58G
COOKING TIME: 15 MINUTES
SERVES: 3
```

INGREDIENTS

- 450g skirt steak
- 60g finely chopped parsley
- 3 finely chopped garlic cloves
- 180ml olive oil
- 15g cup finely ground mint
- 3 tablespoons red wine vinegar
- 2 tablespoons finely chopped oregano
- 1 tablespoon finely ground cumin
- 2 teaspoons paprika, smoked
- 1 teaspoon cayenne pepper
- 1 teaspoon white salt
- ¼ teaspoon black pepper

PROCEDURE

1. Cut the steak into 2 portions – each should be about 225g
2. Combine all the other ingredients in a mixing bowl for the Chimichurri
3. Take ¼ cup of the Chimichurri mixture and put it into a re-sealable bag along with the portions of steak
4. Refrigerate for 2-24 hours and only remove from the refrigerator 30 minutes before cooking
5. Preheat the air fryer to 200°C
6. Pat the steak dry using a paper towel
7. Add the steak to the cooking basket cook for 10 minutes
8. Garnish the steak with 2 tablespoons of the Chimichurri

AIR FRIED HASSEL BACK POTATOES

NUTRITIONAL INFORMATION
CALORIES: 207KCAL
PROTEIN: 2.8G
CARBOHYDRATES: 22.9G
FAT: 12.2G
COOKING TIME: 30 MINUTES
SERVES: 6

INGREDIENTS

- 4 Maris Piper potatoes
- 2 ½ tablespoon olive oil
- Bacon bits
- 60g shredded cheese

PROCEDURE

1. Wash and peel the potatoes
2. Cut the larger potatoes in half
3. Slit the potatoes about 6mm from the base and 5mm apart
4. Preheat the air fryer to 175°C
5. Brush the potatoes with olive oil and toss them into the cooking basket
6. Place the cooking basket into the air fryer and cook for 15 minutes
7. Brush again with olive oil and cook for a further 15 minutes
8. Remove and evenly spread the shredded cheese and bacon bits over the top

CRISPY FRIED SPRING ROLLS

```
NUTRITIONAL INFORMATION
CALORIES: 78KCAL
PROTEIN: 2G
CARBOHYDRATES: 12G
FAT: 1G
COOKING TIME: 20 MINUTES
SERVES: 3
```

INGREDIENTS

For filling

- 112.5g cooked and shredded chicken breast
- 1 thinly sliced medium carrot
- 50g thinly sliced mushrooms
- 1 crumbled chicken stock cube
- 1 teaspoon sugar
- ½ teaspoon finely ground ginger

For spring roll wrappers

- 1 beaten egg
- 8 spring roll wrappers
- 1 teaspoon corn starch
- ½ tablespoon vegetable cooking oil

PROCEDURE

1. Put the cooked and shredded chicken into a bowl then mix with celery, mushrooms and carrot
2. Add the ginger, crumbled chicken stock cube and sugar, then stir thoroughly
3. Combine the beaten egg with corn starch, then mix to bring it to a thick paste. Set it aside

4. Spread some filling onto the spring roll wrapper, then roll it up

5. Use the egg mixture to seal the ends of the rolls

6. Preheat the air fryer to 200°C

7. Lightly brush the spring rolls with oil then place them into the cooking basket and cook in two batches each for about 4 minutes

8. Serve with soy sauce

AIR FRIED FETA TRIANGLES

```
NUTRITIONAL INFORMATION
CALORIES: 107KCAL
PROTEIN: 2G
CARBOHYDRATES: 6G
FAT: 7G
COOKING TIME: 20 MINUTES
SERVES: 4
```

INGREDIENTS

- 112g feta cheese
- 1 egg yolk
- 2 sheets defrosted filo pastry
- 2 tablespoons olive oil
- 2 tablespoons finely chopped parsley
- 1 finely chopped scallion
- 1 pinch ground black pepper

PROCEDURE

1. Beat the egg yolk in a bowl
2. Mix the beaten egg with feta cheese, scallion and parsley
3. Add black pepper for seasoning
4. Cut each filo pastry into 3 strips
5. Scoop a teaspoon full mixture of feta and spread on the underside of the filo pastry strip
6. Fold the tip of the filo pastry to form a triangle folding over the filling
7. Fold in a zigzag manner to ensure all the filling is wrapped in a triangle. Do this for all the filo pastry and feta mixture

8. Preheat the air fryer to 200°C
9. Brush the prepared feta filled filo pastry triangle with olive oil then toss them in a cooking basket. Cook in the air fryer for 3 minutes
10. Preheat the temperature to 180°C and cook for a further 2 minutes
11. Do this for all the feta triangles and serve

AIR FRIED KOREAN BBQ SATAY

```
NUTRITIONAL INFORMATION
CALORIES: 211KCAL
PROTEIN: 30G
CARBOHYDRATES: 8G
FAT: 6G
COOKING TIME: 15 MINUTES
SERVES: 4
```

INGREDIENTS

- 450g skinned, boneless chicken tenders
- 120ml pineapple juice
- 120ml low sodium soy sauce
- 60ml cup sesame oil
- 4 chopped scallions
- 4 garlic cloves
- 1 tablespoon grated fresh ginger
- 2 teaspoon toasted sesame seeds
- 1 pinch black pepper

PROCEDURE

1. Skewer the chicken tenders and trim excess fat or meat
2. In a large mixing bowl combine all the other ingredients
3. Add to the mixing bowl the skewered chicken tenders then mix and refrigerate for up to 24 hours
4. Preheat the air fryer to 200°C
5. Use the paper towel to pat dry the refrigerated chicken tenders
6. Place half of the dried chicken into a cooking basket and cook for 7 minutes

MOROCCAN MEATBALLS WITH MINT YOGHURT

NUTRITIONAL INFORMATION

CALORIES: 524KCAL
PROTEIN: 39G
CARBOHYDRATES: 21G
FAT: 32G
COOKING TIME: 25 MINUTES
SERVES: 4

INGREDIENTS

For meatballs

- 450g lamb, ground
- 225g turkey, ground
- 1 egg white
- 60ml olive oil
- 1 ½ tablespoon finely chopped parsley
- 1 tablespoon finely chopped mint
- 2 garlic finely chopped cloves
- 1 teaspoon red chilli sauce
- 1 teaspoon cayenne pepper
- 1 teaspoon coriander, ground
- 1 teaspoon cumin, ground
- 1 teaspoon salt

For mint yoghurt

- 120ml non-fat Greek yoghurt
- 60g sour cream
- 15g finely chopped mint
- 1 finely chopped garlic clove
- 2 tablespoons buttermilk
- 2 pinches of salt

PROCEDURE

1. Preheat the air fryer to 200°C
2. Combine all the meatball ingredients in a large bowl
3. Roll the meatballs between the palms of your hands in a circular motion to smoothen the meatball into golf ball sizes

4. Place half of them into the air fryer cooking basket and cook each batch for 8 minutes

5. As the meatballs cook in the air fryer, mix the mint ingredients in a mixing bowl and serve with meatballs

6. Bonus tip: Garnish with fresh mint and olives

MAIN DISHES

CHEESY BEEF AND VEGETABLE CASSEROLE

```
NUTRITIONAL INFORMATION
CALORIES: 356KCAL
PROTEIN: 28G
CARBOHYDRATES: 21G
FAT: 15G
COOKING TIME: 20 MINUTES
SERVES: 6
```

INGREDIENTS

- 450g lean ground beef
- 2 chopped shallots
- 4 medium Maris Piper potatoes
- 1 diced medium carrot
- 60g chopped celery stalk
- 60g shredded mozzarella cheese

- 60g grated cheddar cheese
- 15g chopped cilantro
- 3 tablespoon extra-virgin oil
- 1 teaspoon chopped garlic
- 1 pinch salt
- 1 pinch black pepper

PROCEDURE

1. Heat some of the extra virgin oil in a large pan over moderate heat
2. Stir fry the shallots with garlic for 3 minutes
3. Add the ground beef to the shallots and cook further for 8 minutes. Stir occasionally then transfer to a clean plate
4. Heat the remaining oil over the same pan then add potatoes, celery and carrots to it
5. Cook while stirring for 20 minutes, until the mixture becomes tender

6.   Stir in cilantro and season with salt and pepper

7.   Preheat the air fryer temperature to 200°C

8.   Place the mixture into a casserole dish which fits into the air fryer cooking basket

9.   Spread evenly, then top with vegetables, cheddar cheese and mozzarella cheese

10. Cook for 20 minutes, then serve

SPICY ROASTED CHICKEN DRUMSTICKS

NUTRITIONAL INFORMATION
CALORIES: 257KCAL
PROTEIN: 31.4G
CARBOHYDRATES: 0.9G
FAT: 13.6G
COOKING TIME: 20 MINUTES
SERVES: 4

INGREDIENTS

- 450g chicken drumsticks
- 2 tablespoons olive oil
- 2 tablespoons red wine vinegar
- 1 teaspoon onion powder
- ½ teaspoon paprika
- ½ teaspoon ground cumin
- ½ teaspoon dried thyme
- 1 pinch of salt
- 1 pinch of ground pepper

PROCEDURE

1. Preheat the air fryer to 180°C
2. Whisk the red wine vinegar, olive oil, onion powder, thyme, paprika and cumin in a large bowl
3. Place the chicken breasts in a small shallow dish
4. Sprinkle the mixture over the chicken breasts
5. Season with salt and pepper and toss to coat well
6. Cover with plastic wrap to let it marinate for a few minutes
7. Place the marinated drumsticks in a cooking basket and place in the air fryer
8. Cook for 20 minutes and serve

TURKEY MELT SANDWICH

NUTRITIONAL INFORMATION
CALORIES: 294KCAL
PROTEIN: 16.8G
CARBOHYDRATES: 25.3G
FAT: 15.0G
COOKING TIME: 15 MINUTES
SERVES: 4

INGREDIENTS

- 4 slices lean turkey
- 8 slices whole-wheat bread
- 8 slices of tomato
- 4 slices of cheese

PROCEDURE

1. Preheat oven fryer temperature to 180°C
2. Top each slice of bread with cheese, turkey and tomato slices
3. Press two slices of bread together to make a sandwich
4. Place the sandwiches inside a cooking basket and cook in the air fryer for 10-15 minutes

QUICK-ROASTED TOMATO SAUCE WITH CAPERS AND BASIL

```
NUTRITIONAL INFORMATION
CALORIES: 626KCAL
PROTEIN: 18G
CARBOHYDRATES: 103G
FAT: 16G
COOKING TIME: 30 MINUTES
SERVES: 4
```

INGREDIENTS

- ½ punnet of cherry tomatoes
- 1 sliced shallot
- 225g pasta
- 60g cup grated parmesan cheese
- 15g chopped fresh basil

- 2 tablespoons capers
- 2 tablespoons olive oil
- 1 tablespoon white wine vinegar
- 1 teaspoon Italian seasoning

PROCEDURE

1. Preheat the air fryer to 200°C
2. Toss the cherry tomatoes, white wine vinegar, olive oil, capers, garlic, shallots and Italian seasoning in a large bowl and mix them well
3. Add salt and pepper for seasoning
4. Transfer the ingredients into the air fryer and cook for 20 minutes
5. Toss the hot pasta with the air fryer cooked tomato sauce then add the liquid from the bottom drawer of the air fryer to the sauce to thin it
6. Stir in the fresh basil and serve with grated parmesan cheese

AIR FRIED AUBERGINE PARMESAN PANINI

NUTRITIONAL INFORMATION

CALORIES: 883KCAL
PROTEIN: 32G
CARBOHYDRATES: 63G
FAT: 58G
COOKING TIME: 15 MINUTES
SERVES: 4

INGREDIENTS

- 1 medium aubergine
- 3 chopped basil leaves
- 225g mozzarella
- 180g tomato sauce
- 60g breadcrumbs
- 60g mayonnaise
- 2 tablespoons milk
- 2 tablespoons grated parmesan cheese
- 2 teaspoons dried parsley
- ½ teaspoon Italian seasoning
- ½ onion powder
- 1 ½ teaspoon garlic
- 1 pinch black pepper

PROCEDURE

1. Prepare the aubergine slices by salting the sides then lay them between sheets of paper towel
2. Set aside for 20 minutes
3. Prepare a dredging station
4. Mix the garlic, breadcrumbs, onion powder, Italian seasoning, parsley, salt and pepper
5. Whisk mayonnaise and milk together to smoothness
6. Preheat the air fryer to 200°C
7. Brush off any excess salt from the slices of the aubergine

8. Coat each side of the slices with mayonnaise mixture then dip into the breadcrumbs

9. Place the fully coated aubergine slices on a baking tray and spray them with olive oil

10. Air fry the slices for 15 minutes making sure to turn them after seven minutes

11. After cooking the aubergine slices, assemble the panini by first generously applying olive oil on one side of each of the bread slices

12. Place two bread slices on a cutting board with the side containing olive oil facing down

13. Top the two bread slices with a quarter of the mozzarella cheese then sprinkle some parmesan cheese

14. Divide the air fried aubergine between the panini bread, spreading the slices evenly on the cheese

15. Spread tomato sauce on top of the aubergine slices and spread the remaining mozzarella cheese and parmesan cheese

16. Sprinkle chopped basil on the parmesan cheese and then cover with another slice of bread with the oiled surface facing up to make a sandwich

17. Gently pick up the sandwiches and place them on a preheated panini press or contact grill

18. Press down gently to evenly brown both sides of the sandwiches

19. Grill for 10 minutes or until all the cheese is melted and the bread turns brown, to ensure it's well toasted

SUN-DRIED TOMATO STEAKS WITH LEMON HAZELNUT COUSCOUS

NUTRITIONAL INFORMATION
CALORIES: 735KCAL
PROTEIN: 28G
CARBOHYDRATES: 62G
FAT: 40G
COOKING TIME: 40 MINUTES
SERVES: 6

INGREDIENTS

- 450g steak
- 300ml boiling water
- 195g dried lemon hazelnut couscous
- 95g sun-dried and oil-packed tomatoes
- 120ml red wine vinegar
- 25g cup chopped toasted hazelnut
- 60ml olive oil
- 30g chopped fresh parsley

- 1 sliced garlic clove
- 2 tablespoons fresh oregano leaves
- 1 tablespoon fresh chopped lemon zest
- 1 tablespoon fresh lemon juice
- 1 tablespoon butter
- ½ teaspoon salt
- ½ teaspoon ground black pepper

PROCEDURE

1. Cut the steak into sizes that can fit in your air fryer
2. Combine the sun-dried tomatoes with the fresh oregano leaves in a food processor and process them into a marinade paste
3. Add the red wine vinegar and ¼ of the olive oil and process further
4. Transfer the marinade into a re-sealable plastic bag and add the black pepper and sliced cloves of garlic

5. Use a needle style tenderiser to tenderise the steak. You can also use a paring knife to pierce it several times
6. Take the steak, add the marinade ingredients inside the re-sealable plastic bag and allow it to marinate for 2-24 hours in the refrigerator
7. Remove the steak from the bag 30 minutes before cooking
8. Preheat the air fryer to 200°C
9. Season the marinated steak salt and ground black pepper
10. Put the steak into the cooking basket and cook in the air fryer for 10 minutes turning it halfway through the cooking
11. Prepare the lemon hazelnut couscous while the steak is cooking by first placing the dried couscous, lemon zest and a pinch of salt in a heat resistant bowl
12. Pour the 1 ½ boiling water into the bowl and stir once then cover with a lid immediately
13. After 5 minutes, remove the lid and fluff the couscous using a fork knife then add the tablespoon butter, lemon juice, fresh parsley and chopped hazelnuts
14. Remove from the air fryer and let it cool for 5 minutes before serving

Bonus tip: Serve the air fried steak in a whole piece on the bias with lemon hazelnut couscous and green vegetables.

TURKEY BREAST WITH MAPLE MUSTARD GLAZE

NUTRITIONAL INFORMATION

CALORIES: 413KCAL
PROTEIN: 73G
CARBOHYDRATES: 8G
FAT: 9G
COOKING TIME: 60 MINUTES
SERVES: 4

INGREDIENTS

- 1.8kg whole turkey breast
- 60ml maple syrup
- 2 tablespoons Dijon mustard
- 1 tablespoon butter
- 2 teaspoons olive oil

- 1 teaspoon dried thyme
- ½ teaspoon smoked paprika
- ½ dried sage
- ½ freshly ground black pepper
- 1 pinch salt

PROCEDURE

1. Preheat the air fryer to 175°C
2. Brush the turkey breast with olive oil
3. Combine the dried sage, smoked paprika, dried thyme, black pepper and salt. Rub this mixture of spices all over the turkey breast to season it
4. Put the seasoned turkey breast into the cooking basket and cook in the air fryer for 25 minutes
5. Turn the turkey breast on its side inside the air fryer and cook for 12 more minutes then turn it again onto the opposite side and cook it for 12 minutes again

6. Take a small saucepan and combine the maple syrup, Dijon mustard and butter for a nice glaze

7. Turn the turkey breast in an upright position and brush the glaze all over it then cook for 5 final minutes until it turns nicely brown

8. Before serving, tent the turkey loosely with a foil and let it rest for 5 minutes

KING PRAWNS IN HAM WITH RED PEPPER DIP

NUTRITIONAL INFORMATION
CALORIES: 317KCAL
PROTEIN: 42G
CARBOHYDRATES: 6G
FAT: 17G
COOKING TIME: 25 MINUTES
SERVES: 4

INGREDIENTS

- 10 frozen and defrosted king prawns
- 1 large red bell pepper
- 5 slices of raw ham
- Tapas fork

- 1 large crushed garlic clove
- 1 tablespoon olive oil
- ½ tablespoon paprika
- ½ teaspoon ground black pepper

PROCEDURE

1. Preheat the air fryer to 200°C
2. Put the red bell pepper into the cooking basket and slide it into the air fryer
3. Set the timer to 10 minutes and roast the red bell pepper until the skin becomes slightly charred
4. Remove the charred bell pepper and place it in a bowl. Cover it with a lid and allow it to rest for 15 minutes
5. Peel the prawns and remove the black vein at the back
6. Slice into half lengthwise then use the slices to wrap the prawns
7. Coat every ham wrapped prawn with olive oil and toss into the cooking basket

8. Set the air fryer timer to 3 minutes then slide the cooking basket in and cook until the prawns become crispy

9. While the prawns are cooking, remove the red bell pepper from the bowl and peel off the skin. Remove the seeds and cut into pieces

10. In a blender, puree the red bell pepper with paprika, garlic and some olive oil. Pour the blended sauce onto a dish and season with salt and black pepper

11. Serve the air fried ham wrapped prawns on a platter with a tapas fork and seasoned red bell pepper sauce

ROASTED RACK OF LAMB AND CRUST OF MACADAMIA

```
NUTRITIONAL INFORMATION
CALORIES: 435KCAL
PROTEIN: 26G
CARBOHYDRATES: 2G
FAT: 36G
COOKING TIME: 40 MINUTES
SERVES: 4
```

INGREDIENTS

- 0.84kg rack of lamb
- 1 beaten egg
- 60g unsalted macadamia nuts
- 1 garlic clove
- 1 tablespoon olive oil
- 1 tablespoon chopped fresh rosemary
- 1 tablespoon breadcrumbs
- 1 pinch salt
- ½ teaspoon pinch black pepper

PROCEDURE

1. Finely chop the garlic cloves and add olive oil to make garlic oil
2. Brush the rack of lamb with the garlic oil and season with a pinch of salt and black pepper
3. Preheat the air fryer to 120°C
4. Chop the unsalted macadamia nuts finely and place in a bowl
5. Add rosemary and the breadcrumbs to the bowl of macadamia nuts and stir
6. In another bowl whisk the egg

7. Dip the seasoned rack of lamb into the egg and then into the bowl containing the macadamia crust

8. Place the coated rack of lamb into the cooking basket and toss the basket into the air fryer

9. Set the air fryer to 25 minutes and let the rack of lamb cook for the set time then increase the temperature to 200°C and cook for 5 more minutes

10. Remove from the air fryer and cover with aluminium foil for 10 more minutes before serving

AIR FRIED STICKY BBQ PORK STRIPS

```
NUTRITIONAL INFORMATION
CALORIES: 305KCAL
PROTEIN: 35.3G
CARBOHYDRATES: 1.5G
FAT: 16.6G
COOKING TIME: 25 MINUTES
SERVES: 3
```

INGREDIENTS

- 6 pieces tenderised pork loin chops
- 1 clove garlic
- 2 tablespoons soy sauce
- 2 tablespoons honey
- 1 teaspoon balsamic vinegar
- ½ teaspoon freshly ground black pepper
- ¼ teaspoon finely ground ginger

PROCEDURE

1. Season the tenderised pork chops with ground black pepper
2. Pour the honey, soy sauce and balsamic vinegar into a bowl to make a marinade
3. Add the chopped garlic and ground ginger into a bowl, then stir thoroughly and set aside
4. Place the marinade mixture into a re-sealable plastic bag and add the pork chops to marinate them
5. Let it marinate in a refrigerator overnight
6. Set the air fryer to 175°C
7. Remove the pork chops with the marinade mixture from the plastic bag 30 minutes before cooking and place it inside the cooking basket
8. Let it cook and turn it on each side for every 5 minutes until all the pork chops turn golden brown

SPICY FISH STREET TACOS WITH SRIRACHA SLAW

```
NUTRITIONAL INFORMATION
CALORIES: 877KCAL
PROTEINS: 38G
CARBOHYDRATES: 87G
FAT: 42G
COOKING TIME: 20 MINUTES
SERVES: 4
```

INGREDIENTS

- 360g mahi mahi or snapper fish fillets
- 6 inch flour tortillas
- 1.5kg shredded green cabbage
- 125g breadcrumbs
- 60g mayonnaise
- 60g flour
- 30g shredded carrots
- 60ml milk
- 2 chopped scallions
- 1 egg beaten
- 1 lime cut into wedges
- 2 tablespoons Sriracha slaw
- 2 tablespoons rice vinegar
- 1 tablespoon olive oil
- 1 teaspoon sugar
- 1 teaspoon chilli powder
- 1 teaspoon salt
- ½ teaspoon baking powder
- ½ teaspoon ground cumin
- ½ teaspoon ground black pepper

PROCEDURE

1. In a large mixing bowl, combine the mayonnaise, sugar, Sriracha slaw sauce and rice vinegar
2. Add the green cabbage, chopped scallions and shredded carrots
3. Mix well and toss to ensure all the vegetables are thoroughly coated with pepper and salt, then refrigerate the slaw until the tacos are ready

4. In a clean bowl, combine cumin powder, flour, chilli powder, salt, pepper and baking powder

5. Add egg and milk to the mixture and mix well to get a smooth batter

6. Put the breadcrumbs into a shallow dish

7. Slice the fish fillets into sticks of 2.5cm each

8. Toss the fish fillet sticks into the smooth batter to coat it and let the excess drip off before dipping them into the breadcrumbs

9. Set the coated fish fillet stick on a baking tray and then finish coating all the other fish fillets

10. Preheat the air fryer to 200°C

11. Spray the coated fish fillet sticks on all the sides with olive oil

12. Place all the sticks in a single layer in the cooking basket leaving some little space around each stick

13. Air fry the coated fish fillet sticks for 3 minutes then turn them. Air fry for another 2 minutes

14. Warm your tortilla shells wrapped in foil in a 175°C oven. You can also warm in a skillet with a little oil over medium-high heat for some 2-3 minutes

15. Fold the tortillas in half

16. Make your tacos by wrapping two air-fried coated fish fillet stick with the tortilla shell

17. Top with Sriracha sauce and squeeze a lime wedge over the top to serve

AIR FRIED DUCK BREAST WITH ROASTED FIG AND POMEGRANATE MOLASSES

NUTRITIONAL INFORMATION

CALORIES: 596KCAL
PROTEINS: 46G
CARBOHYDRATES: 80G
FAT: 11G
COOKING TIME: 60 MINUTES
SERVES: 4

INGREDIENTS

- 450g boneless duck breast
- 6 halved fresh figs
- 480ml fresh pomegranate juice
- 3 tablespoons brown sugar
- 2 tablespoons olive oil
- 2 tablespoons lemon juice
- 1 teaspoon salt
- ½ teaspoon freshly ground black pepper
- 2 sprigs of fresh thyme

PROCEDURE

1. Prepare the pomegranate molasses by combining the pomegranate juice with lemon juice and brown sugar in a medium saucepan
2. Heat the mixture and bring it to boil
3. Lower the heat and simmer the mixture for 25 minutes until it becomes thick enough to coat the back of a spoon
4. Preheat the air fryer to 200°C
5. Using a sharp knife slit the duck breast diagonally across the skin. This should render any fat
6. Make four additional slits across the skin in the opposite diagonal direction
7. Season the duck breast using salt and the freshly ground black pepper

8. Place the duck breast with the skin facing up into the air fryer and air fry for 10 minutes

9. Turn the duck breast and air fry for an additional 5 minutes

10. Flip the duck breast again to the skin side up position and air fry for 1 minute. Transfer to a chopping board

11. Drizzle some olive oil over the figs and season with freshly ground black pepper and salt

12. Toss the figs into the air fryer and let them fry for 5 minutes

13. Slice the air fried duck breast on the bias and drizzle the warm pomegranate molasses over the top

14. Garnish with sprigs of thyme and serve with the roasted figs

AIR FRIED FALAFEL

CALORIES: 60KCAL
CARBOHYDRATES: 9.9G
PROTEINS: 3.1G
FATS: 1.1G
COOKING TIME: 30 MINUTES
SERVES: 6

INGREDIENTS

For Falafel

- 800g canned chickpeas (rinsed and drained)
- 5g coriander
- 5g packed parsley
- 4 cloves garlic
- ½ medium yellow onion (cut into quarters)

- 1 teaspoon baking powder
- 1 teaspoon dried coriander
- 1 teaspoon cumin
- 1 teaspoon salt
- ½ teaspoon chilli flakes

For tahini sauce

- 80g tahini
- 3 tablespoon water
- ½ squeezed lemon (juice)

- 1 pinch salt
- 1 pinch chilli flakes

PROCEDURE

1. Put the onion, clove garlic, coriander leaves and parsley in a food processor, scraping down the sides as much as needed
2. Add the drained chickpeas, baking powder, salt, coriander powder, chilli flakes and cumin

3. Pulse again to break the chickpeas down with some chunks and only stop when the mixture turns into a paste

4. Add salt and pepper for seasoning

5. Scoop 2 tablespoons of the mixture and gently squeeze into a ball being careful not to squeeze too much. Do this to form balls with all the remaining mixture

6. Place a few balls into the air fryer and cook for 15 minutes at 190°C

7. While the Falafels are cooking in batches, prepare the tahini sauce by combining tahini and lemon juice in a medium bowl

8. Add water and stir to combine it well and continue adding water if necessary to achieve the desired consistency

9. Season with a pinch of salt and chilli flakes to taste

10. Serve the falafels with the tahini sauce in a pitta or a salad

AIR FRIED ROASTED VEGETABLE PASTA SALAD

```
NUTRITIONAL INFORMATION
CALORIES: 37KCAL
PROTEINS: 1.4G
CARBOHYDRATES: 3.4G
FAT: 2.4G
COOKING TIME: 25 MINUTES
SERVES: 6
```

INGREDIENTS

- 120g mushrooms
- 450g cooked penne or rigatoni
- 90g cherry tomatoes
- 95g pitted Kalamata olives
- 5 tablespoons olive oil
- 1 zucchini cut into half moons
- 1 yellow squash sliced into half moons
- 1 large green pepper
- 1 large orange pepper
- 1 large red pepper
- 1 sliced red onion
- 3 tablespoons balsamic vinegar
- 2 tablespoons fresh basil
- 1 teaspoon Italian seasoning
- 1 teaspoon salt
- ½ teaspoon freshly ground black pepper

PROCEDURE

1. Preheat the air fryer to 193°C
2. Place the red pepper, orange pepper, green pepper, zucchini, yellow squash, mushrooms and red onions in a large bowl
3. Add some drizzles of the olive oil and toss to coat well
4. Season with salt, ground black pepper and Italian seasoning
5. Put in the cooking basket and air fryer for 15 minutes or until the vegetables become soft, but not mushy

6. Shake or stir halfway through the cooking time to ensure the vegetables are evenly roasted

7. In another large mixing bowl, combine the cooked penne or rigatoni, Kalamata olives, grape tomatoes and the roasted vegetables

8. Add the balsamic vinegar and toss well

9. Add olive oil and stir to coat it well

10. Season with salt and the ground black pepper

11. Refrigerate until when you are ready to serve

12. Stir in the fresh basil just before serving

AIR FRIED TERIYAKI SALMON

```
NUTRITIONAL INFORMATION
CALORIES: 276KCAL
PROTEINS: 29G
CARBOHYDRATES: 13G
FAT: 10G
COOKING TIME: 15 MINUTES
SERVES: 2
```

INGREDIENTS

- 180g salmon
- 4 tablespoons soy sauce
- 110g brown sugar
- 6 tablespoons rice wine vinegar
- 2 crushed garlic cloves
- 1 teaspoon grated ginger

PROCEDURE

1. Combine soy sauce, brown sugar, red wine vinegar, garlic and ginger in a pan
2. Heat teriyaki sauce until sugar dissolves
3. Soak salmon in teriyaki sauce for a minimum of 20 minutes to overnight
4. Make a shallow dish out of aluminium foil
5. Place marinated salmon in an aluminium dish
6. Place salmon into the air fryer cooking basket
7. Place the basket in the air fryer and cook at 175°C for 7 minutes
8. Remove basket from air fryer and top the salmon with marinade
9. Place the basket in the air fryer and cook at 175°C for 7 more minutes

AIR FRIED LEMON MAHI MAHI

NUTRITIONAL INFORMATION
CALORIES: 91KCAL
PROTEINS: 5.6G
CARBOHYDRATES: 1.6G
FAT: 7.3G
COOKING TIME: 25 MINUTES
SERVES: 4

INGREDIENTS

- 180g mahi mahi
- 2 tablespoons butter
- 6cm lemon slice
- 1 teaspoon white salt

PROCEDURE

1. Wash and rinse the mahi mahi
2. Place the mahi mahi in an aluminium foil dish
3. Top dress with butter
4. Put the lemon slices on top of the mahi mahi
5. Place aluminium dish with mahi mahi into the air fryer cooking basket
6. Place the basket into the air fryer and cook at 175°C for 14 minutes
7. Season with salt to taste

SPICY ROASTED CHICKEN DRUMSTICKS

```
NUTRITIONAL INFORMATION
CALORIES: 257KCAL
PROTEINS: 31.4G
CARBOHYDRATES: 0.9G
FAT: 13.6G
COOKING TIME: 20 MINUTES
SERVES: 4
```

INGREDIENTS

- 450g chicken drumsticks
- 2 tablespoons olive oil
- 2 tablespoons red wine vinegar
- 1 teaspoon onion powder
- ½ teaspoon paprika
- ½ teaspoon dried thyme
- ½ teaspoon ground cumin
- ½ teaspoon fresh ground black pepper
- ½ teaspoon salt

PROCEDURE

1. Preheat the air fryer to 180°C
2. Whisk the red wine vinegar, paprika, cumin, dried thyme, onion powder and olive oil in a small bowl
3. Place the chicken drumstick in a separate shallow dish and drizzle the whisked olive oil mixture from the small bowl
4. Toss to coat well and season with salt and ground black pepper
5. Cover it and let it marinate for at least 20 minutes
6. Place the marinated chicken drumstick inside the air fryer and cook for 20 minutes

TERIYAKI GLAZED HALIBUT STEAK

NUTRITIONAL INFORMATION
CALORIES: 240KCAL
PROTEINS: 25.2G
CARBOHYDRATES: 16.6G
FAT: 7.5G
COOKING TIME: 30 MINUTES
SERVES: 3

INGREDIENTS

- 450g halibut steak
- 1 smashed clove of garlic
- 160g soy sauce
- 120ml Mirin (Japanese cooking wine)
- 50g sugar
- 60ml orange juice
- 2 tablespoons lime juice
- ½ teaspoon crushed red pepper flakes
- ½ teaspoon ground ginger

PROCEDURE

1. In a saucepan, combine smashed clove garlic, ginger, lime juice, orange juice, sugar, red pepper flakes, Mirin and soy sauce for the teriyaki glaze/marinade
2. Add salt for seasoning
3. Bring the mixture to a boil and reduce by half, then set aside to cool
4. Once cooled pour half of the glaze/marinade into a re-sealable bag with the halibut steak
5. Refrigerate for at least 30 minutes to allow it to marinate well
6. Preheat the air fryer to 200°C

7. Remove the marinated halibut from the refrigerator some minutes prior to placing it into the air fryer

8. Cook for 10 minutes

9. When cooked properly, remove from the air fryer and brush a little of the remaining glaze over the air fried halibut steak

AIR FRIED WHOLE CORNISH HEN

NUTRITIONAL INFORMATION
CALORIES: 300KCAL
PROTEINS: 25G
CARBOHYDRATES: 34G
FAT: 21G
COOKING TIME: 30 MINUTES
SERVES: 4

INGREDIENTS

- 1 Cornish hen
- 120ml olive oil
- 1 lemon zest
- 1 teaspoon chopped thyme
- 1 teaspoon chopped rosemary
- ¼ teaspoon crushed red pepper flakes
- ¼ teaspoon salt
- ¼ teaspoon sugar

PROCEDURE

1. Place the Cornish hen on a cutting board and with the back of the hen facing you, use a boning knife to cut from the top to the bottom of the backbone, making 2 cuts on either side of the backbone to remove the backbone
2. Split the hen lengthwise by cutting through the breastplate
3. Take the two halves of the hen and set them aside
4. In a large mixing bowl combine the salt, lemon zest, olive oil, chopped rosemary, chopped thyme, sugar and red pepper flakes for the marinade
5. Add the two halves of the hen to the marinade
6. Refrigerate for 1 hour up to 24 hours to properly marinate

7. Preheat the air fryer to 200°C

8. Remove the hen from the marinade and drain off any liquid. Pat dry with a paper towel

9. Put the marinated chicken halves into the cooking basket and cook for 15 minutes

AIR FRIED CHICKEN TENDERS

NUTRITIONAL INFORMATION

CALORIES: 25KCAL
PROTEINS: 26.2G
CARBOHYDRATES: 9.8G
FAT: 11.4G
COOKING 30 MINUTES
SERVES: 2

INGREDIENTS

- 450g chicken breast tenders
- 2 large eggs
- 125g panko breadcrumbs
- 60g finely shredded parmesan cheese
- 30g all-purpose flour
- 2 tablespoons Italian seasoning
- 1 teaspoon salt
- 1 teaspoon garlic powder

PROCEDURE

1. Combine the parmesan, breadcrumbs, garlic powder, salt and Italian seasoning in the shallow dish
2. Pour all-purpose flour in a separate shallow dish
3. Beat eggs and pour into another shallow dish
4. Coat the chicken tenderloins in flour, shaking off any excesses
5. Dip each flour-coated chicken tenderloin in egg and let any excess drip off
6. Roll the chicken tenderloins in the breadcrumb mixture
7. Place the coated chicken tenderloins in the air fryer and ensure that there is only a single layer with little space between each tenderloin
8. Cook at 150°C for 30 minutes
9. Remove chicken tenders from the air fryer basket and serve with the dipping sauce of your choice

Bonus Recipes

AIR FRIED FISH FILLETS

NUTRITIONAL INFORMATION
CALORIES: 314KCAL
CARBOHYDRATES: 27G
PROTEINS: 37G
FATS: 6G
COOKING TIME: 15 MINUTES
SERVES: 4

INGREDIENTS

- 120g breadcrumbs
- 4 white fish fillets
- 1 lemon, sliced
- 1 egg, beaten

PROCEDURE

1. Preheat the air fryer to 180°C
2. Put the breadcrumbs in a mixing bowl and mix with oil
3. Stir the mixture to make it loose and crumbly
4. Pour the egg into a shallow dish and dip the fish fillets into the egg
5. Shake off any excesses and dip into the breadcrumbs and ensure an even coating
6. Lay the breadcrumb coated fish fillets in the air fryer and cook for about 12 minutes
7. Garnish with lemon slices and serve

AIR FRYER CHICKEN THIGHS

NUTRITIONAL INFORMATION
CALORIES: 243KCAL
CARBOHYDRATES: 0.2G
PROTEINS: 27G
FAT: 16G
COOKING TIME: 60 MINUTES
SERVES: 6

INGREDIENTS

- 4 chicken thighs
- 80ml low sodium soy sauce
- 60ml extra virgin olive oil
- 1 squeezed lemon (juice)
- 2 cloves garlic crushed

- 2 tablespoon chilli garlic sauce
- 2 tablespoon honey
- 2 teaspoon freshly grated ginger
- Toasted sesame seeds
- Thinly sliced spring onions

PROCEDURE

1. Mix the soy sauce, honey, lime juice, chilli garlic, and ginger in a large bowl
2. Reserve 120ml of this marinade and add the chicken thighs to the bowl then toss to coat well
3. Refrigerate for 30 minutes
4. Remove the bowl from the refrigerator 30 minutes before cooking time and take out 2 thighs from the marinade. Place them in the air fryer
5. Cook the thighs in the air fryer at a temperature of 200°C until the thighs are cooked with an internal temperature of 73°C for 20 minutes
6. Take the cooked thighs out of the air fryer and tent with aluminium foil
7. Take the remaining 2 thighs from the marinade and repeat the procedure

8. Bring the reserved 120ml marinade to boil over medium heat in a small saucepan

9. Lower the heat and simmer the marinade sauce to thicken it for 5 minutes

10. Brush the thighs with the sauce

11. Garnish with spring onions and sesame seeds to taste then serve

AIR FRYER ROTISSERIE CHICKEN

```
NUTRITIONAL INFORMATION
CALORIES: 166KCAL
CARBOHYDRATES: 1G
PROTEIN: 28.4G
FAT: 6.4G
COOKING TIME: 50 MINUTES
SERVES: 6
```

INGREDIENTS

- 1.3kg chicken
- 1 tablespoon dried thyme
- 2 teaspoon garlic powder
- 2 teaspoon onion powder
- 2 teaspoon dried oregano
- 1 teaspoon paprika
- ¼ teaspoon cayenne

PROCEDURE

1. Drizzle the salt and pepper all over the chicken to season it
2. Mix and whisk the spice mixture of dried thyme, oregano, onion powder, paprika, cayenne and garlic
3. Rub the spice mixture all over the chicken pieces
4. Put dark meat pieces into the air fryer basket and set the temperature to 180°C then cook for 10 minutes
5. Flip and cook for additional 10 minutes
6. Now take the chicken pieces and cook in the air fryer for 8 minutes each side
7. Use a meat thermometer to ensure the chicken cooks with an internal temperature of 73°C

DESSERTS

AIR FRIED CHOCOLATE BROWNIES

NUTRITIONAL INFORMATION
CALORIES: 385KCAL
PROTEINS: 6G
CARBOHYDRATES: 54G
FAT: 18G
COOKING TIME: 20 MINUTES
SERVES: 3

INGREDIENTS

- 170g brown sugar
- 160ml milk
- 113g butter
- 125g caster sugar
- 120g self-rising flour
- 60g chocolate
- 2 medium eggs, beaten
- 2 sliced bananas
- 2 tablespoons vanilla essence
- 2 tablespoons water

PROCEDURE

1. Preheat the oven air fryer to 175°C
2. Melt 85g of the butter and chocolate in a bowl, over medium heat
3. Stir in the brown sugar
4. Add the beaten eggs and then the vanilla essence
5. Add the self-rising flour and mix thoroughly
6. Pour the dough into a greased dish and place it into the air fryer
7. Cook for 15 minutes
8. Prepare the caramel sauce by mixing the caster sugar with the water in a saucepan over medium heat until the sugar melts
9. Turn up the heat and cook for 3 more minutes for the mixture to turn a little brown

10. Turn off the heat and let the melted sugar rest for 2 minutes then add the remaining butter and stir until it all melts
11. Add the milk to the mixture gradually
12. Take the caramel sauce and set it aside to allow it to cool
13. The brownies in the air fryer should be ready now, so take them out and chop them into squares
14. Place them on a plate with sliced bananas and top them with the caramel sauce

CHOCOLATE PROFITEROLES

NUTRITIONAL INFORMATION

CALORIES: 390KCAL
PROTEINS: 7G
CARBOHYDRATES: 45G
FAT: 27G
COOKING TIME: 20 MINUTES
SERVES: 2

INGREDIENTS

- 125g plain flour
- 6 medium eggs, beaten
- 110g butter
- 2 tablespoons vanilla essence
- 2 tablespoons icing sugar
- 120g milk chocolate
- 2 tablespoon whipped cream

PROCEDURE

1. Preheat the air fryer to 170°C
2. Place ¾ of the butter in a large pan over medium heat and allow it to boil
3. Remove from the heat and stir in the flour then return it to the heat until it forms a dough
4. Set the dough aside and let it cool
5. Add in the eggs and mix to create a smooth consistency
6. Mould into profiteroles and cook in the air fryer for 10 minutes at 175°C
7. Make cream filling by whisking vanilla essence with icing sugar and whipped cream until nice and thick

8. Prepare the chocolate topping by placing chocolate, the remaining butter and cream in a glass bowl

9. Mix well to melt all the chocolate

10. Remove the profiteroles from the air fryer and top with the chocolate to serve

PARMESAN DUSTED GARLIC KNOTS

NUTRITIONAL INFORMATION
CALORIES: 37KCAL
PROTEINS: 1G
CARBOHYDRATES: 5G
FAT: 2G
COOKING TIME: 15 MINUTES
SERVES: 3

INGREDIENTS

- 400g refrigerated pizza crust
- 3 tablespoons minced garlic
- 3 tablespoons olive oil
- 2 tablespoons parmesan cheese powder
- 1 pinch garlic salt

PROCEDURE

1. Roll the refrigerated pizza crust on the cutting board
2. Cut into 0.6cm strips
3. Wrap the strips into knots
4. Mix olive oil and garlic in a bowl to form garlic oil
5. Dip the knots into the garlic oil
6. Place the knots on a plate and dash with garlic salt
7. Transfer the knots into the cooking basket, 12 of them at a time
8. Set the timer to 4 minutes at a temperature of 200°C
9. Let them cook and remove once the cooking time counts down
10. Dust with parmesan cheese powder to serve

APPLE CINNAMON DESSERT EMPANADAS

```
NUTRITIONAL INFORMATION
CALORIES: 191KCAL
PROTEINS: 6G
CARBOHYDRATES: 52G
FAT: 6G
COOKING TIME: 25 MINUTES
SERVES: 2
```

INGREDIENTS

- 12 empanada wrappers
- 2 diced apples
- 2 tablespoons corn starch
- 2 tablespoons raw honey
- 1 tablespoon cinnamon

- 1 tablespoon vanilla extract
- 1 tablespoon olive oil
- 1 tablespoon water
- ½ teaspoon nutmeg

PROCEDURE

1. Combine the nutmeg, honey, cinnamon, vanilla and apples in a saucepan and cook over medium-high heat. Stir for 3 minutes, until the apples are soft
2. Mix corn starch and water in a small bowl. Add this to the saucepan, stir and cook for 30 seconds
3. Lay the empanada wrappers on a flat surface and place the apple mixture onto it
4. Close the empanadas and roll halfway
5. Pinch the crust along the edges of the wrapper and roll the sides inwards until the crust is closed

6. Place the wrapped empanada contents into the air fryer and cook at 200°C for 8 minutes

7. Turn and flip the empanadas and cook for 10 more minutes

8. Remove from the air fryer and serve the apple cinnamon dessert empanadas

MIDNIGHT NUTELLA BANANA SANDWICH

NUTRITIONAL INFORMATION
CALORIES: 388KCAL
PROTEINS: 7G
CARBOHYDRATES: 61G
FAT: 7G
COOKING TIME: 10 MINUTES
SERVES: 2

INGREDIENTS

- 60g softened butter
- 4 slices bread
- 1 banana
- 4 tablespoons of chocolate hazelnut spread

PROCEDURE

1. Preheat the air fryer to 180°C
2. Spread the softened butter on one side of the bread slices
3. Place the slices on the counter with the butter side facing down
4. Spread the hazelnut on the top facing sides of the bread slice
5. Cut the slices into half and split the halves lengthwise into 3 strips
6. Place the strips on two slices of bread and then top with the remaining two slices to form two sandwiches
7. Cut the sandwiches into half so they can fit into the air fryer
8. Place them into the air fryer and cook for 5 minutes at 180°C
9. Flip them and cook for 3 more minutes

AIR FRIED STUFFED APPLE PIES

NUTRITIONAL INFORMATION
CALORIES: 633KCAL
PROTEINS: 7G
CARBOHYDRATES: 89G
FAT: 49G
COOKING TIME: 20 MINUTES
SERVES: 2

INGREDIENTS

- 4 sour apples
- 2 sweet apples
- 2 ready-made pie dough slices
- 1 lemon
- 1 egg, beaten

- 3 tablespoons sugar
- 2 tablespoons butter
- 1 teaspoon ground cinnamon
- ¼ teaspoon ground ginger
- 1 pinch nutmeg

PROCEDURE

1. Cut off the tops of the sour apples
2. Use a paring knife to cut the inside edge of the apple leaving a 0.6cm inch border of apple next to the skin
3. Scoop out the inside of the apple with a spoon and set it aside
4. Discard the core and seeds of the apple and squeeze the lemon juice inside the apple
5. Preheat a skillet over medium heat
6. Add the butter to the skillet
7. Sauté apple pulp with diced apples, sugar, cinnamon, ginger and nutmeg for 3 minutes
8. Fill the apple shells with the sautéed apple mixture

9. Cut the pie dough into 16 strips of 2.5cm by 10cm inches each

10. Lay 2 strips across the top of each apple

11. Interweave the other 2 strips in the opposite direction over the apple

12. Brush the dough strips with the beaten egg and sprinkle the sanding sugar on top

13. Preheat the air fryer to 175°C

14. Place the stuffed apples in the air fryer and cook for 10 minutes

STRAWBERRY SCONES

NUTRITIONAL INFORMATION
CALORIES: 361KCAL
PROTEINS: 7G
CARBOHYDRATES: 55G
FAT: 12G
COOKING TIME: 20 MINUTES
SERVES: 4

INGREDIENTS

- 125g self-rising flour
- 100g caster sugar
- 120ml milk
- 60g fresh strawberries
- 4 tablespoons whipped cream
- 3 tablespoons butter
- 1 tablespoon vanilla essence
- 1 tablespoon strawberry jam

PROCEDURE

1. Combine the flour, sugar and butter in a mixing bowl
2. Add more butter to the sugar and flour to resemble breadcrumbs
3. Add vanilla essence and milk to soften the dough
4. Mould 4 equal sized balls
5. Place the scone dough onto a baking tray and put into the air fryer
6. Cook for 10 minutes at 175°C
7. Once cooked, allow it to cool and cut them in half
8. Fill the halved scones with strawberries, strawberry jam and whipped cream

PEANUT BUTTER MARSHMALLOW FLUFF TURNOVERS

```
NUTRITIONAL INFORMATION
CALORIES: 249KCAL
PROTEINS: 3.9G
CARBOHYDRATES: 41.8G
FAT: 8.3G
COOKING TIME: 20 MINUTES
SERVES: 4
```

INGREDIENTS

- 4 sheets filo pastry, defrosted
- 60g butter, melted
- 4 tablespoons chunky peanut butter
- 4 teaspoons marshmallow fluff
- 1 pinch sea salt

PROCEDURE

1. Preheat the air fryer to 180°C
2. Brush 1 sheet of filo with melted butter
3. Put the second sheet of filo on top of the first and brush again with butter
4. Do the same for all the remaining filo sheets
5. Cut the filo layers into 4 7cm x 30cm strips
6. Place 1 tablespoon of peanut butter and 1 teaspoon of marshmallow fluff on the underside of a strip of filo
7. Fold the tip of the sheet over the filling to form a triangle and fold repeatedly in a zigzag manner until the filling is fully wrapped
8. Use a touch of butter to seal the ends of the turnover
9. Place the turnovers into the cooking basket and cook for 3-5 minutes, until golden brown and puffy
10. Finish with a pinch of sea salt for a sweet and salty combination

AIR FRIED VANILLA SOUFFLÉ

INGREDIENTS

- 240ml whole milk
- 240g egg whites
- 4 egg yolks
- 60g all-purpose flour
- 60g softened butter
- 50g sugar
- 2 teaspoons vanilla extract
- 1 teaspoon cream of tartar
- 1 vanilla bean

PROCEDURE

1. In a mixing bowl add the flour and butter and mix to form a smooth paste
2. Heat the milk in and dissolve in the sugar
3. Into the milk solution, add the vanilla bean and allow it to boil
4. Take the flour and butter mixture and add into the boiling milk and use a wire whisk to beat vigorously to ensure there are no lumps
5. Simmer for several minutes to thicken the mixture
6. Remove the mixture from the heat and discard the vanilla bean then set aside to let the mixture cool for 10 minutes in an ice bath
7. While the mix is cooling, take 6 90g ramekins or soufflé dishes and coat them with butter and sprinkle a pinch of sugar
8. Beat the egg yolks in another mixing bowl and add the vanilla extract

9. Combine with the egg yolk mixture with the cooled milk mixture

10. Beat the egg whites, tartar cream and sugar and until the egg whites form medium-stiff peaks

11. Take the egg whites mixture and fold it into the milk and egg yolk mixture then put into the soufflé dishes

12. Place in baking dishes and smooth off the tops

13. Preheat the air fryer to 167°C

14. Place 2 or 3 soufflé dishes into the cooking basket and cook each batch for 12-15 minutes

15. Dust with powdered sugar on top of the soufflé and serve with chocolate sauce on the side

Disclaimer

This book contains opinions and ideas of the author and is meant to teach the reader informative and helpful knowledge while due care should be taken by the user in the application of the information provided. The instructions and strategies are possibly not right for every reader and there is no guarantee that they work for everyone. Using this book and implementing the information/recipes therein contained is explicitly your own responsibility and risk. This work with all its contents, does not guarantee correctness, completion, quality or correctness of the provided information. Misinformation or misprints cannot be completely eliminated.

Printed in Great Britain
by Amazon